G ABOUT SEX

How You Are Changing

for **Girls**

ages **10-12**

and parents

CONCORDIA PUBLISHING HOUSE · SAINT LOUIS

For Discussion or Individual Use

Book 3 of the
Learning about Sex Series for Girls

The titles in the series:

Book 1: *Why Boys and Girls Are Different*

Book 2: *Where Do Babies Come From?*

Book 3: *How You Are Changing*

Book 4: *Sex and the New You*

Book 5: *Love, Sex, and God*

Book 6: *How to Talk Confidently with Your Child about Sex*

Acknowledgments

We wish to thank all medical, child development, and family life consultants who have assisted in the development, updating, and revising of the Learning about Sex series.

Copyright © 1982, 1988, 1995, 1998, 2008 Concordia Publishing House
3558 S. Jefferson Ave., St. Louis, MO 63118-3968

1-800-325-3040 • www.cph.org

From text originally written by Jane Graver

Illustrations by Len Ebert

Scripture quotations, unless otherwise indicated, are taken from THE HOLY BIBLE, NEW INTERNATIONAL VERSION®. NIV®. Copyright © 1973, 2978,1984 by International Bible Society. Used by permission of Zondervan Publishing House. All rights reserved.

Scripture quotations marked ESV are from The Holy Bible, English Standard Version®. Copyright © 2001 by Crossway Bibles, a publishing ministry of Good News Publishers, Wheaton, Illinois. Used by permission. All rights reserved.

The Bible text in the publication marked TEV is from the Good News Bible, the Bible in TODAY'S ENGLISH VERSION. Copyright © American Bible Society 1966, 1971, 1976. Used by permission.

This publication may be available in Braille, in large print, or on cassette tape for the visually impaired. Please allow 8 to 12 weeks for delivery. Write to Lutheran Blind Mission, 7550 Watson Road, St. Louis, MO 63119-4409; call 1-888-215-2455; or visit the Web site: www.blindmission.org.

Manufactured in China

1 2 3 4 5 6 7 8 9 10   17 16 15 14 13 12 11 10 09 08

Contents

Editors' Foreword 5

A Note to Parents 6

1. You Are Wonderful 11

2. Male + Female + God's Gift of Life = BABY 15

3. God Took Care of You . . . Right from the Beginning 25

4. You've Grown! 35

5. Next Step: Adolescence 39

6. Am I Normal? 45

7. Feeling Good about Your Sexuality 49

8. It's Great to Be Alive! 53

Some Words Used in This Book 56

Editors' Foreword

This book is one of a series of six designed to help parents communicate biblical values to their children in the area of sexuality. *How You Are Changing* is the third book in the series. It is written especially for girls ages 10 to 12, and, of course, for the parents, teachers, and other concerned grown-ups who may want to discuss the book with the children in their care. (See "A Note to Parents" at the beginning of this book for suggestions on using the book and ways to communicate Christian values in sex education in the home.)

Like its predecessor, the new Learning about Sex series provides information about the social-psychological and physiological aspects of human sexuality. Moreover, it does so from a distinctively Christian point of view, in the context of our relationship to the God who created us and redeemed us in Jesus Christ. The series presents sex as another good gift from God, which is to be used responsibly.

Each book in the series is graded—in vocabulary and in the amount of information it provides. It answers the questions that children at each age level typically ask.

Because children vary widely in their growth rates and interest levels, parents and other concerned adults will want to preview each book in the series, directing each child to the next graded book when she is ready for it.

In addition to reading the books, parents can use them as starting points for casual conversation and when answering other questions children might have.

The books in this series also can be used as mini units or as part of another course of study in a Christian school setting. Whenever the books are used in a class setting, it is important to let the parents know beforehand, since they have the primary responsibility for the sex education of their children. If used in a classroom setting, the books in this series are designed for separate, single-gender groups, the setting most conducive to open conversations about questions and concerns.

While parents will appreciate the help of the school, they will want to know what is being taught. As the Christian home and the Christian school work together, Christian values in sex education can be more effectively strengthened.

The Editors

A Note to Parents

After you read this book, you may feel quite puzzled. Is all this factual information really necessary for 10- to 12-year-olds? It's probably a lot more than we knew when we were that age.

Our children are living in a different world than the one in which we grew up. They are exposed to distorted information about sex every day—through TV shows, movies, the Internet, the words to popular music, and from their friends at school (Christian schools too). If they already have a solid foundation of knowledge and attitudes, they can evaluate the improper values and the misinformation they get from other sources instead of accepting whatever they hear or learning only as a reaction to a negative situation.

Research has shown that children are far more likely to develop healthy attitudes about their sexuality when parents encourage discussions about sex. Too much information does not seem to do any harm when linked to positive values. The child who feels unable to ask questions is far more likely to become preoccupied with sex than the one who has open access to information.

Of course, girls from ages 8 to 11 will vary widely in their ability to understand the material in this book. You are the best judge of what is appropriate for your own child at each stage of her development. To decide whether this book is too advanced or too easy for your daughter, examine *Where Do Babies Come From?* and *Sex and the New You,* the books that come immediately before and after *How You Are Changing* in this series.

How should you use this book? We recommend that you either read it with your daughter or let her read it, and then discuss sections about which she has questions. Most children will not want to read all of it at once. They will probably be interested in different sections at different stages of their development. Another option is to use the book as a "what to say" resource as you talk with your daughter.

Ideally, this book is part of a much more broadly focused yet more personal training of young girls for biblical womanhood. Young women grow and blossom into Christian womanhood through the teaching, training, and example provided by older women. A young woman can learn much from a mother, grandmother, or other adult who trusts in Jesus for her salvation. In the context of such a relationship, questions of a personal nature can be asked and answered, insightful discussions held, and godly behaviors modeled. Your expression of positive and God-pleasing values will likely have a greater impact on the healthy development of your daughter than any book, other than the Bible. God's plan unfolds as each generation in succession passes on the truths God imparts through His Word and the wisdom that comes as challenges are met and overcome by the power of God's grace through Jesus Christ, our Savior and Lord.

We have a reason for suggesting that sex education begin at an early age. Nearly all the young adults we questioned about their memory of the sex education they had in their own homes said something like "Too little, too late. It turned me off to have to listen to a bunch of stuff I already knew—or thought I knew."

Where did these parents go wrong? In many cases they were waiting for questions, ready with carefully planned answers. Sometimes no questions came. Did that mean their children weren't interested? Of course not. Perhaps the children had sensed their parents' discomfort. Or maybe they had learned from others that sex is a subject some people prefer not to discuss.

If talking about sex is difficult for you, it might be a good idea to tell your child about your feelings. You could say something like "This is so special, so private, that I'm a little uncomfortable talking about it. But thank you for asking such a good question; that really helps."

You will find that once trust, genuineness, and openness are established, it will be easier for everyone. Your child will learn better and remember more from a series of shorter conversations than from a long, serious talk that may be put off because of the difficulty of finding the right time and place for it.

Speaking of time and place, be ready for some surprises. When you show your child that it's okay to talk about sex, she'll ask questions whenever and wherever she happens to think of them.

Many young people who criticized their parents as sex educators admitted that the parents' attitudes and values came through, in spite of their clumsiness in expressing them. It's comforting to know that we can make mistakes without necessarily ruining our children, isn't it? Somehow God blesses our bumbling efforts and makes them work far better than we would have dreamed possible.

How to Use This Book

1. You can sit down and read all of the book at once, or you can use the contents section to look up questions you may have. It's a good idea to talk over what you learn with an adult you can trust, and to pray about your discussions.

2. Some pages have pictures with labels on them. Be sure to study the pictures and read the labels very carefully.

3. "Some Words Used in This Book" (see page 56) can help you understand and pronounce the technical words you'll find in this book.

4. When you see this kind of print: *Says who?*—that's what someone might say to the writer of this book. The same kind of print is used for the prayers in this book, because they are what someone might say to God.

1

You Are Wonderful

Says who?

Says God, that's who. He knows you, and He thinks you are terrific.

How do I know He doesn't have me mixed up with some other kid?

God made you different from every other kid in the whole world. In fact, you are different from every other kid who has ever lived! Your fingerprints and your footprints are different from those of any other person. Nobody else has your special mix of hair color, freckles, talents, likes and dislikes, and the million other things that make you you. When God made you, He made one of a kind.

Hey, wait a minute. God made Adam and Eve. But I was born. I came from my mother and father.

That's right. But God was there blessing you. Life comes only from God. Your life is a gift from Him, a gift with your name on it.

God knows you. He knows everything about you. And He loves you just as you are. That's not the same as loving everything you do.

We are human beings and are all sinners. Sadly, we know that sin has been part of our human nature ever since sin first entered the world. But once again, God is there blessing us. God gives life—new life, eternal life—through Jesus to all who believe in Him as Savior. You are wonderful! You are a child of God.

You Are a Female

God created people to be female or male. *Female* and *male* are the words we use to describe a person's **sex**. Your sex is a very important gift from God. Because you are a female, you can be a mother someday. What other differences are there between being a female and a male?

These differences are not just physical. Pediatric nurses in hospitals often note that newborn babies already indicate distinctiveness, with baby girls tending to focus eye contact on a person, while baby boys seem to look all over to take in the big picture. These differences do not mean that one sex is better than the other. They just mean that God made female and male with gender-related characteristics we can celebrate and thank God for.

People need one another and are a blessing to one another. God's view of female and male is not of a difference that competes, separates, or conflicts. Rather it is God-pleasing when our unique abilities and per- spectives support each other. 1 Corinthians 11:11 (ESV) says, "In the Lord woman is not independent of man nor man of woman." Key words that God desires in a harmonious boy/girl or man/woman relationship  include encouragement, respect, cooperation, sharing, and caring.

There are differences between girls and boys and between women and men, but there are many ways that all people are alike. These are factors that relate to humanness, rather than femaleness or maleness. One way we are all the same is that we are loved by God and saved through faith in Jesus. Galatians 3:28 (ESV) says, "There is neither Jew nor Greek, there is neither slave nor free, there is no female and male, for you are all one in Christ Jesus." This does not say we are the same. It says that though each is distinct, one is not better than the other. All who are in Christ have equal standing before God and an equal share of the inheritance in heaven He has obtained for us.

Your Feelings Are Important

Meredith loved to run and often entered children's races. When Meredith was in a race, she put everything she had into winning.

Then someone called Meredith a "tomboy." She didn't want to be different from other girls she knew, so she stopped racing. As she watched the boys run, Meredith told herself she didn't miss racing at all.

But it wasn't true. And she felt so unhappy about giving up racing that she had trouble making friends.

Meredith needs to listen to her own feelings and not worry so much about what other people say. If she remembers that God loves her just as she is and that God has blessed her with a talent for running, it will be easier for her to like herself.

Not everyone understands that girls and boys have some of the same feelings. Leon's dog, Rex, was killed by a car. Whenever Leon thought about Rex, he just couldn't help crying—even though he had been told, "Big boys don't cry."

Now Leon felt even worse, because he was afraid people might call him a "sissy." He was ashamed to feel so sad after Rex's death. He told himself, "Rex was a dumb old dog and I don't even miss him." When Leon locked his sad feelings inside himself, his stomach hurt. Lying to himself just made him feel worse.

Leon should understand that it is normal for a person to cry when he feels sad. (Even Jesus cried. Read about it in John 11:32–35.) People who try to be too tough to cry often become unable to show *any* feelings—love and joy as well as sadness. The bottled-up feelings make them unhappy, some-times even sick.

Leon would probably feel better if he went off by himself and cried when he felt like it. Or he might say to himself, "Yes, I really feel sad, but if I get busy doing something interesting, maybe my sad feelings will go away." Most of all, Leon needs to remember that he can tell *Jesus* how he feels. Jesus knows how we feel, for He grew up as a human being just like us (except, of course, without sin).

God blesses us with many talents and abilities that are related not to femaleness or maleness but to our humanness. Some girls like to play soccer or fix bicycles; other girls would rather be cheerleaders or take dancing lessons. Some boys love to draw or play the piano; other boys would rather play baseball or build birdhouses.

Thank God you have these choices. God has given you many, many talents to which you can bring your uniqueness as a female. If you try a lot of different activities, you will discover many things you are good at, things that make you special. And if you have many different interests, you will have many more ways of making friends. Praise God that He created us—male and female—in His image (Genesis 1:27, 31), an image that is being restored in us through the grace and mercy of Christ Jesus. (See 2 Corinthians 3:18 and Romans 12:2 to learn about how God transforms us!)

Remember, He loves you no matter what. So just be yourself, the terrific person God made.

God made you a girl. He will help you grow into a happy woman.

> Jesus grew in wisdom and stature, and in favor with God and men. (Luke 2:52)
>
> For we do not have a high priest who is unable to sympathize with our weaknesses, but we have one who has been tempted in every way, just as we are—yet was without sin. (Hebrews 4:15)
>
> Jesus went throughout Galilee, teaching in their synagogues, preaching the good news of the kingdom, and healing every disease and sickness among the people. (Matthew 4:23)

You were a child once, Jesus. Like me, You learned as You grew up. You chose not to be selfish and mean, but You were still a real person. You and Your friends hiked from one city to another, helping people. You were brave and independent—and You also were gentle and kind. You loved everyone—and You still do, the Bible says.

Do You really love me, Jesus? Even when I back away instead of trying something hard? When other kids make fun of me, I need to know You think I'm special. Give me the courage to grow to be more like You—and to remember that You love me even when I fail. Thank You for forgiving my sins. Be with me, Jesus, as I grow up.

2

Male + Female
+ God's Gift of Life = Baby

Women and Men: Alike, Yet Different

If you could see inside the bodies of a woman and a man, you would find much that is alike. In both women and men the heart pumps blood and the lungs breathe. Many other **organs** work together to keep the person alive.

What are organs?

Body parts like the heart, brain, and lungs are called organs. **Sexual organs** do the work of creating new life. They are different in women and men.

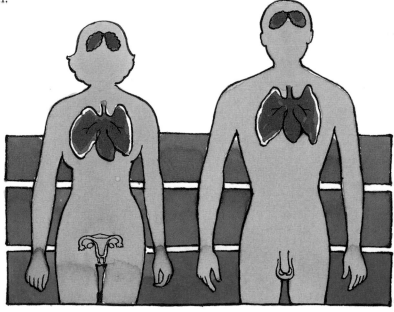

When you began life, you were just one tiny cell, smaller than the dot of an i. This tiny cell that was you was formed when an egg cell from your mother joined with a sperm cell from your father.

Under a strong microscope they'd look about like this:

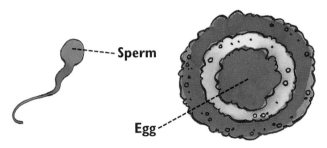

How great God must be, to make a whole person grow from such a tiny beginning! Everyone you know began life in the very same way. That is part of why God made women and men different from each other. Both are needed to bring new life into the world. Both are needed to love, protect, and guide the child they have begun.

A Woman's Sexual Organs

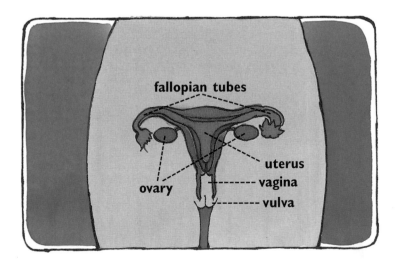

The egg cell from which you grew was made in your mother's **ovary**. A woman has two ovaries deep inside her body, a little lower than her waist. Each one is only as big as an almond, yet thousands of egg cells are stored there.

When a girl is between the ages of 10 and 14 (sometimes a little earlier, sometimes a little later) the egg cells in her ovaries begin to change and ripen. After that, about once a month, an egg cell leaves one of the ovaries.

Near each ovary, a hollow tube, called a **fallopian tube**, opens to receive the egg. While passing through this tube, the egg may meet and unite with a sperm. If it unites with a sperm, the egg continues its journey to the **uterus**. If it does not join a sperm, the egg disintegrates.

The uterus lies between the ovaries and just above the bone that forms a bridge between a girl's legs. It is about the size and shape of a pear. This organ can stretch like a balloon to many times its ordinary size. It is here that a fertilized egg cell grows into a baby.

The uterus is connected to the outside of the body by a narrow passage-way. This organ, the **vagina**, opens between the legs. It is covered by folds of skin and flesh called the **vulva**. The opening through which urine passes is also within the vulva. The **anus**, where bowel movements leave the body, is behind the vulva.

The ovaries, fallopian tubes, uterus, vagina, and vulva are the **reproductive organs** of girls and women. All except the vulva are inside the body.

A Man's Sexual Organs

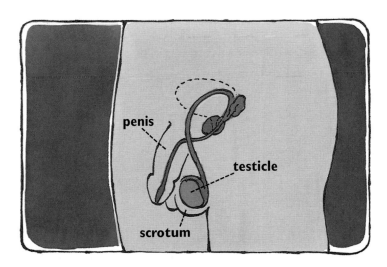

penis

testicle

scrotum

The sperm cell from which you grew was made in one of your father's **testicles**. There are two roundish testicles in a bag of skin called the **scrotum**. The scrotum hangs just behind and under a man's **penis**. The penis is a finger-shaped organ, which is usually soft and spongy.

In the testicles of a grown man, billions of sperm cells grow each month. They are stored in a tube that is in the back of the testicles.

When a boy becomes old enough (approximately between ages 12 and 15), his testicles begin to make sperm cells. His body also makes a milky liquid in which the sperm cells swim. The sperm cells and the milky liquid in which they swim are called **semen**. Semen leaves the body through the penis.

Urine (waste water) also passes from the body through the penis but never at the same time as semen. The **anus**, where bowel movements leave the body, is behind the testicles.

A Brand-New Person

When an egg cell in one of your mother's fallopian tubes met and united with a sperm cell from your father, your life began. In that instant, the question of whether you were going to be a girl or a boy was decided. There are many sperm cells in a man's semen. About half of them are able to start a girl baby; about half are able to start a boy baby. It all depends on which sperm cell joins the egg cell.

The egg cell and the sperm cell did more than just stick together. Following God's design, the two cells changed into one *new* cell—the beginning of a brand-new person! That tiny life has all the DNA factors that make a person unique—that make you *you*.

The speck of new life was female; it had in it the color of your hair, the shape of your nose, and the talents that would someday help make you special. That's why you look a little bit like your mother and a little bit like your father.

Then why isn't my hair curly like my dad's? And why are my eyes blue when both my parents have brown eyes?

A woman's body makes thousands of egg cells in her lifetime. Each of those egg cells has different **genes**, different directions for making a baby. A man makes billions of sperm cells in his lifetime; each one has different genes in it. Your **characteristics**, things like straight hair and blue eyes, were decided by the particular genes in the sperm cell that happened to join the genes in a particular egg cell.

Grandpa and I like to go fishing. Did I get "go fishing" genes from him?

Maybe. Your genes might make you more likely to be a person who is good at catching fish. But your experiences—the fun you have with Grandpa or the time you caught that big fish—are also important in making you the person you are.

Your effort is important too. You probably try hard to follow Grandpa's directions when you fish together.

Your experiences, your learning, and your hard work will always be an important part of you. You can't change the color of your eyes, but you can become a better reader. You can learn to control your quick temper.

Everyone is born with both strengths and weaknesses. With God's help, you can discover your strengths—your best characteristics—and work to develop them. And, with God's help, you can learn ways to overcome or compensate for your weaknesses.

You Are an Important Part of a Family

Your family is another of God's gifts to you—and you are God's gift to your family.

Me? God's gift to my family?

That's right. Whether you are the oldest child or a middle one or the youngest, your family would not be complete without you.

Then why do I get blamed for everything?

Very likely your sister or brother would ask the same question. In every family, each child sometimes thinks someone else is the parents' favorite.

The fact is that parents do not treat all their children in the same way, because each child is a unique individual with different abilities, concerns, and problems. Parents treat each child a little differently because each child is special. Your parents probably try hard to meet your individual needs.

Families begin when a man and woman decide to get married. They plan to live their lives together. They promise to be together and take care of each other for as long as they live. This is God's plan, as Jesus states in Mark 10:6–9 (ESV), that "from the beginning of creation, God made them male and female. Therefore a man shall leave his father and mother and hold fast to his wife, and the two shall become one flesh. So they are no longer two but one flesh. What therefore God has joined together, let not man separate."

A husband and wife are to be "best friends" who trust each other and support and respect each other. They ask God to help them be honest with each other. Each knows the other will try to understand, responding with loving-kindness and forgiveness.

But sometimes my parents fight.

How about you? Do you always get along with your best friend?

We-l-l-l . . .

Exactly. We are all sinners—grown-ups too. Because Jesus died for us and rose again, we can ask our heavenly Father to forgive us. And we can ask God's Spirit to help us grow as Christians. We can listen to the other person's side. We can try harder to consider the other person's feelings. We can be more honest about our own feelings. We can forgive each other.

Even though a husband and wife promise to be best friends, they have to keep working to make their friendship better. In a good marriage, they feel so close to each other they are almost like one person. (This is what Jesus means when He says they become one flesh.) What hurts one hurts the other. What blesses one blesses the other.

Not all families have a mother and a father.

Yes, that's true. Sometimes sad things happen, like death or divorce. Children in these families often feel that whatever happened must be partly their fault. But there is nothing a child can do to stop such things from happening. There is no way a child can make divorced people want to get married again.

It's important to remember that *all* families have hard times. God is there in good times and in bad. He is always ready to forgive us and to bless us in ways we might not even expect.

No family is perfect. People are never exactly as we would like them to be. But God will help you accept the people in your family as they are. He will help you love and support each other. He will help your love grow. 1 John 4:11 reminds us, "Since God so loved us, we also ought to love one another."

God's Plan for New Life

A woman and a man get married because they love each other very much. Each of them has found a special friend, much better than any friend they have ever had. And they *show* their love in many ways. They help each other. They share happy times and sad times. They enjoy just being together. Each married couple has their own favorite ways of showing love for each other.

At times, a husband and wife will want to express their love for each other in a special way called sexual **intercourse**. At those times, they will go off by themselves. They will hug and kiss each other and touch each other all over. The husband's penis will become firm and hard, able to fit inside his wife's vagina. This is to be a private act between husband and wife.

While they are loving each other in this way, semen comes out of the husband's penis. Many sperm cells are in the semen. The sperm cells move up the vagina, through the uterus, and into the fallopian tubes leading to the ovaries. If one sperm cell joins an egg cell in a fallopian tube, new life begins. A baby is started.

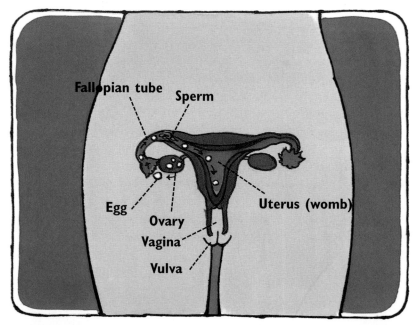

A baby does not begin to grow every time a husband and wife have intercourse. An egg cell is in one of the fallopian tubes only a few days each month, and only then can a baby be started.

God wants only a wife and her husband to make love in this way. People who are not married who have intercourse are breaking God's commandments (Exodus 20:14). They have turned away from God's will and put their own will above God's. This is sinful and leads to many troubles. When books, movies, TV shows, and even some "friends" say this is okay, we should remember that God comes first in our lives and so we obey Him. He knows what is best for us.

Husbands and wives have promised to live together always and to make a home for their children. As parents, they will take care of the babies born to them.

Some people decide not to have any children. Some others cannot have children because their sexual organs do not work as they should. Some couples without children want children enough to adopt children whose birth parents could not take care of them. They are usually very good parents who love their adopted children very much.

> The word of the LORD came to me, saying, "Before I formed you in the womb I knew you, before you were born I set you apart." (Jeremiah 1:4–5a)

I don't know, God; this all sounds pretty strange to me. Why did You invent such a complicated way of starting babies? Sure, I'd like to have children of my own someday . . . but I can't imagine wanting to be that close to anyone.

I guess I can see that it would be really nice to have an extra-special friend, someone I could tell anything to and he would understand. Someone who would love me no matter what. Someone who would be there when I need him. When the right time comes, please bless me with a special man to marry—someone who will love me and love You.

Thank You for the friends I have now, God. Teach me to be the kind of friend I'd like to have. Help me get ready for the day when I begin a friendship with my husband—a friendship so special it will last for the rest of my life.

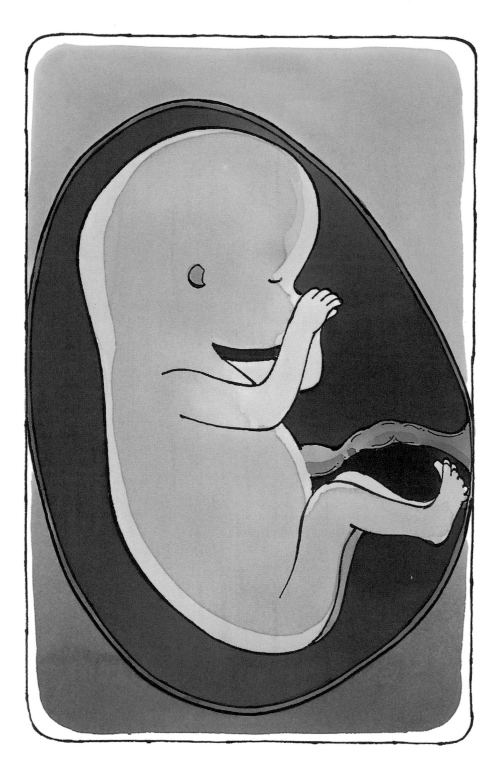

3
God Took Care of You . . . Right from the Beginning

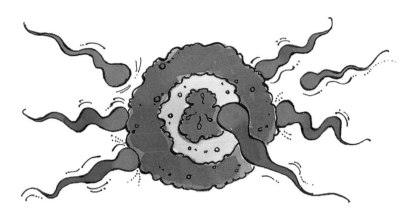

Smaller Than a Dot

When the sperm cell from your father joined the egg cell in your mother, you were really smaller than the dot on this i.

Soon something wonderful happened. That one new cell that was you divided into two cells. All at once you were twice as big as you had been.

During the next few weeks, you doubled your size again and again. You also moved from the fallopian tube to the uterus, where God had prepared a safe and comfortable place for you to live and grow. (See the drawing on page 22.)

At about two months, you were little more than an inch long. On page 24 is an enlarged picture so you can see what you looked like. Do you see the eyes and ears? Your head was very big compared to your body because so much was already developing there. You had short arms and legs and fingers and toes. You had the beginnings of a stomach and a brain.

You Were Safe and Warm and Well-Fed

You floated in a bag full of a liquid that was mostly water. The water acted like a springy cushion, protecting you from bumps. You were always just warm enough. Very hot days or cold days didn't bother you a bit.

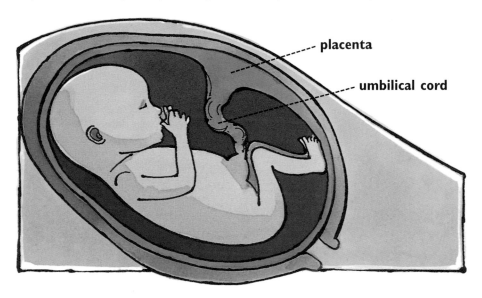

placenta

umbilical cord

Of course, you couldn't eat and breathe in the water the same way you eat and breathe now. Do you see the cord that goes to the baby's navel (belly button)? It is called an umbilical cord. The other end of the cord joins the **placenta**, an organ on the wall of the uterus.

Your blood flowed into the placenta. Food and oxygen moved from your mother's blood to yours. Waste materials from your body went into your mother's bloodstream so your mother could get rid of them. You were sharing your mother's body.

When you had been growing for about four and a half months, you began acting like a newborn baby. You began to suck your thumb, so you would know how to suck for milk after you were born. Still inside the bag of water, you were big enough to push against the walls of the uterus as you kicked and stretched your arms and legs. For the first time, your mother felt a little flutter inside her when you moved. What a thrilling moment that was for her!

Most **pregnant** women have a checkup about once a month to see how the baby is getting along. (The word *pregnant* means that a woman has a baby growing in her uterus.) In time you were big enough for the doctor to hear your heartbeat with a stethoscope. With a special machine, doctors can see how the baby is developing (growing) in the uterus. The picture, or image, seen on the machine is called a sonogram. The doctor or technician can take a picture to show the baby to the mother and father and brothers and sisters. The sonogram can also show whether the baby is a girl or a boy.

The Last Few Months before Birth

As you grew still bigger, your mother's belly, also known as the abdomen, became big and round. Her uterus stretched to give you more room, but you had to lie more and more tightly curled up. Your mother knew when you were asleep, because when you were awake you kicked harder against the wall of the uterus.

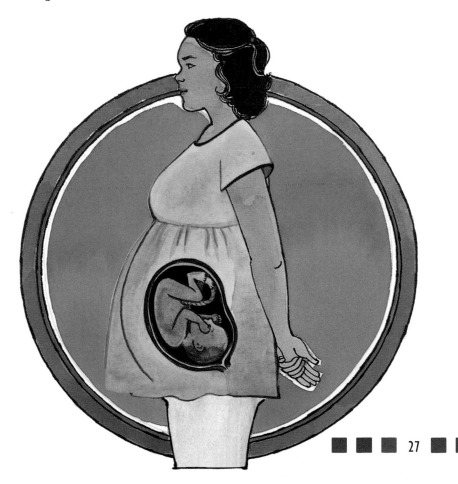

Although your eyes were still tightly shut, your ears were beginning to work. Loud noises made you jump, and you listened all day to your mother's heartbeat. Sometimes you even had hiccups. The people in your family felt the way you do when you are waiting for Christmas. They could hardly wait for you to be born. They asked all sorts of questions: Will our baby be a girl or a boy? Whom will she or he look like? What name shall we choose?

Everyone helped get ready for the big day. Your parents probably fixed a special place for you to sleep. They got baby clothes and diapers and little blankets ready. Your father and sisters and brothers tried to be extra helpful, so your mother could get extra rest. She got tired carrying you around all day!

Your mother packed a little suitcase of clothes for both of you. She wanted to be ready when the time came to go to the hospital where you would be born.

Finally, the Great Day Came

After about nine months, you were ready to be born. The uterus began to squeeze and push you out, very gently at first and then with more and more power. Slowly you moved down into the vagina and out through the vulva.

The bag of water broke, and the vagina and vulva stretched to let you come out between your mother's legs.

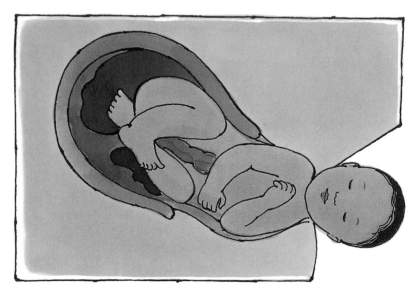

This was very slow, hard work for your mother. The muscles that squeezed and stretched got very tired, so tired they may have hurt. But your mother was happy and excited because she was about to see you for the first time. The long months of waiting were almost over. Soon she would hold you in her arms.

Although it is possible for a mother to give birth to a healthy baby all by herself, most babies are born in hospitals. The doctors and nurses help make the mother and baby more comfortable. The baby's father often helps too.

The mother and the father want to hold the baby as soon as possible, but first the doctor must make sure that the baby is breathing. Usually the baby begins to cry, and no wonder! The baby is still wet from the bag of water, and the room is much colder than the mother's body was.

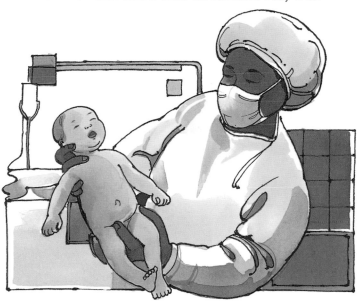

Once the baby begins breathing, it no longer needs the placenta or the umbilical cord. So the doctor cuts the cord. Cutting the cord doesn't hurt the mother or the baby; it's like cutting hair or fingernails.

Soon after the baby is born, the mother's uterus pushes out the placenta. The mother's uterus, vagina, and vulva slowly return to their normal size.

Soon the mother's breasts will begin to make milk. In most cases there will be enough milk to feed the baby for a long time. When the baby no longer sucks at the mother's breasts because he or she drinks from a bottle or a cup, the mother's breasts will stop making milk.

Most babies are not very pretty right after they are born. Often the head has been pushed into an odd shape during birth. The skin is wrinkled and red. After a few days, the skin becomes a normal color and the soft bones of the head move back into shape. But the family usually thinks their baby is beautiful, right from the first day!

Human babies are helpless long after birth. Babies need not only food, warmth, and safety, but also love. A baby who is never held or talked to would probably get sick and might even die. When babies are older, they still need someone who will love them and help them learn and grow. That's why God's plan for families is so important. Babies and children need parents who will love and care for them for many years.

Twins

Once in a while a mother will have two or more babies on the same day. Her uterus will stretch enough to make room for them as they grow. Sometimes the uterus gets too crowded; then these babies are born a little early. Of course, two babies can't come out at the same time, so one is always a few minutes older than the other.

There are two kinds of twins, **fraternal twins** and **identical twins**.

Fraternal twins begin life when two different sperm cells join two different egg cells. Fraternal twins are not much more alike than any other two children in the same family. They might be two boys, two girls, or a boy and a girl.

Identical twins begin life when one sperm cell joins one egg cell. The one new cell splits into two cells, which then grow to become two babies. Identical twins look exactly alike, but they are not. Each one is special. Each has her or his own interests, ideas, personalities, and experiences.

Premature Babies

After nine months in the uterus, babies are ready to live in the world. Babies born before they have been in the uterus nine months are called **premature** babies. They can grow to be strong and healthy—but they need extra care after they are born. They are usually kept for a while in **incubators**, which keep them warm and away from germs.

Taking Care of Our Bodies

What a great responsibility it is to be pregnant! God entrusts a *whole new life* to the mother. Whatever the mother does affects the unborn baby. That's why it's so important for the mother to take care of her own body, especially when she's pregnant. Mothers-to-be should not smoke, drink alcohol, or take drugs because these can cause serious harm to an unborn baby. Whatever the mother takes into her body is shared (unfortunately in some cases) with her baby.

For instance, doctors have learned that an unborn baby's heart beats much faster after the mother smokes a cigarette. When pregnant women smoke, they can do serious damage to the health of their babies. Similarly, babies and children suffer harmful effects when living in a household where one or both parents smoke.

You already know that you feel better and look better if you eat right, get enough sleep and exercise, and stay away from drugs that might be harmful. Now you have another reason to take care of your body. If you decide to have a child someday, you will already have formed the good habits that will help everyone in your family enjoy good health.

> **When my bones were being formed,**
> **carefully put together in my mother's womb,***
> **when I was growing there in secret,**
> **you knew that I was there—**
> **you saw me before I was born.**
> **(Psalm 139:15–16a TEV)**
>
> * Womb is another word for uterus.

Lord, You have taken care of me all my life. You have always been right here . . . close to me, loving me, ready to listen. You know me better than I know myself. How wonderful You are!

Do You remember the day I was born, God? I know You were there. I wish I could remember. What did I notice first in this strange new world? What did my family say, I wonder, when they saw me for the first time?

Yes, You remember the day I was born—and the days before that. If You knew me when I was a tiny speck inside my mother, You surely know me now. You know my likes and dislikes.

You know whether I feel terrific or terrible . . . and You care. You can even look into the future and see the grown-up person I will be someday.

I don't understand how You can know me so well, God, and still love me. But I'm sure glad You do. And I know You love me because You sent Your Son, Jesus, to be born in our sinful world and to die on the cross to take away my sins. Because of Jesus, I know we will be together now and forever in heaven.

4

You've Grown!

Not really. Lots of people in my class are much taller than I am.

The most important growing happens inside a person. You'll grow on the outside, too, when your body is ready. But I know that you are growing on the inside right now.

What do you mean?

When you came to know Jesus, God made you a member of His family. Now, as you learn more about Jesus, you are growing as a Christian.

When you were a little baby, you needed lots of things and you cried and yelled until you got them. Your family gave you food and toys and love. What did you give them? Nothing but a smile.

Now that you are older, you are able to give as well as take. And Jesus helps you. So you do things like setting the dinner table or taking care of younger children when your parents are busy. You notice when they are tired and try to help them. You make a special birthday card for someone you love or just surprise him or her with an extra hug.

Sometimes I don't want to be with my family. I'd rather be alone or with my friends.

That's a part of growing. When you were a baby, you wanted to be with your mother all the time. Even when you began to go to school, it was hard to be away from home so much of the day.

But now you like to stay all night at a friend's house. Maybe you've even gone somewhere—like to a camp—by yourself, even though none of your friends were going. Or maybe your family moved, and you went to a new school where you didn't know anyone.

Going alone was hard. It seemed like everyone had a friend to be with, everyone but me. It made me glad to know that Jesus is my friend!

Did you feel alone for a long time?

It seemed like forever while it was happening. But now that I look back on it, I see that it didn't take long for me to make friends.

Would you go alone again?

It depends. If it's something I really want to do, I'd go alone. Camp, for instance, is so much fun, I can put up with the lonesomeness of the first day.

That's another way you have grown up. When you were little, you couldn't wait for things to get better. If little children are asked to choose between ice cream right now and a new bike next month, they pick the ice cream most of the time.

You know what? I gave up my after-school free time every day for two weeks. I wanted to work on my science fair project: The Human Body. It turned out great! It was worth all that time.

Lots of people your age are interested in the human body and how it works. God made your body beautiful and good and interesting—all of it.

We-l-l-l, there are some parts that aren't so nice. I didn't put sexual organs in my science fair model. People would have said it was dirty and not appropriate.

Your sexual organs are private, not dirty. That's why you cover them up, and also why you do not allow anyone else to touch them. Some people have mixed-up and sinful ideas about sex, but you know better.

You can feel good about your body because you know God created it. You can thank God for its creation in words God's people have used for thousands of years: "I praise You because I am fearfully and wonderfully made; Your works are wonderful, I know that full well" (Psalm 139:14).

God will help a Christian to give her body the best of care. God will guide her to respect her body as He wishes her to. God will lead her to respect other people too.

Some kids sure think sex is dirty. They write words on the bathroom walls, and they tell jokes that make me feel uncomfortable. Half the time I don't get it, but I usually laugh anyway.

As we said, some people have mixed-up and sinful ideas about sex. They might be embarrassed by using the right words for penis and vagina, for instance, so they use slang words instead. Or they get their information from jokes and made-up stories instead of from an adult they can trust, like a parent. We are reminded in Matthew 15:19 (ESV) that "out of the heart come evil thoughts . . . sexual immorality." But we also know that as we are justified by Jesus' saving actions and we are sanctified by the working of the Holy Spirit, God leads us to new life. That allows us to follow the advice of the apostle Paul: "Whatever is true, whatever is honorable, whatever is just, whatever is pure, whatever is lovely, whatever is commendable, if there is any excellence, if there is anything worthy of praise, think about these things" (Philippians 4:8 ESV).

I'd be embarrassed to ask my parents about sex—and I think they'd be embarrassed too.

Maybe. It's a little hard to talk about something that is so private, such a special part of your life. It gets easier, though, the more you talk to your parents. And it's smart to talk about important things with people who care enough about you to make sure you get everything straight.

> **Grow in the grace and knowledge of our Lord and Savior Jesus Christ. To Him be glory both now and forever! Amen. (2 Peter 3:18)**

Dear Lord, I'm growing. In some ways I'm growing too fast, and in some ways I'm growing too slow.

Help me not to be so worried. The too-fasts, too-slows, too-smalls, and too-bigs are based less on facts and more on my feelings. I know, thankfully, that this is all in Your hands.

Lord, You know what is best for me, and Your timing is always best. After all, You said, "I know the plans I have for you . . . plans to prosper you and not to harm you, plans to give you hope and a future" (Jeremiah 29:11).

Someday I'll be grown up—in due time. Help me to focus beyond growing up physically. Guide me throughout my whole life to grow emotionally, socially, intelligently, and above all, spiritually.

Each day, lead me to look to You, dear Lord, as the one who created, redeemed, and comforts me in body and soul.

5
Next Step: Adolescence

A Time of Change

The years when a person changes from a child to an adult are called **adolescence**. Although we think of adolescents as teenagers, some people begin this time of change as early as 9 or 10.

Lots of children find it hard to believe that they will ever be interested in the other sex. The idea of changing into a grown-up person seems very strange to them. But whether they like the idea or not, those who tell them they will change are right. In a few years, girls will probably begin to like boys in a new and special way. When a girl is near a certain boy, she may feel uncomfortable and happy and shy and excited—all at the same time. A boy is likely to have the same feelings when he's with a special girl. Strong feelings are a part of these growing-up years. One day you might feel on top of the world; the next day you might feel very unhappy.

If you have an adolescent brother or sister, you know that people of this age are often hard to live with. They may burst into tears or slam doors for no reason that anyone else can see. They are so busy growing up, they may forget to be patient with younger children in the family. Sometimes they are unpredictable—you don't know what to expect next.

Adolescents usually want more independence than their parents are ready to give them. It's hard for them to wait until parents are convinced they are responsible enough to handle more freedom.

How Girls Change

When a girl begins to grow up, the shape of her body changes. Her breasts and hips slowly become larger. Hair grows near her sexual organs and under her arms. Within one to three years, she might be six to eight inches taller and quite a bit heavier.

About two years after her breasts begin to develop, another important change takes place. An egg cell will move from one of her ovaries to her uterus. Her body sends extra blood to the uterus, so it will be ready to feed the new life that would begin if that egg cell should join a sperm cell. A soft new lining grows all over the inside of the uterus.

When no baby is started, the egg cell, the new lining, and the extra blood aren't needed. They break up and flow out though the vagina. This is called **menstruation**, and it happens about once a month to nearly every woman. The unneeded material is mostly blood, and that's what it looks like. Since we think of being hurt when we see blood, menstruation can be scary for a girl who does not understand what is happening. Remember, this is all *extra* blood that your body does not need, and it comes out very

slowly. These changes are the creation and blessing of God, and we should respect the unique growth and development of every individual.

A woman's **period** (the time when she is menstruating) lasts about three to seven days. It often takes several years before a young girl has a period every month. At first there might be several months between her periods.

When you start menstruating, use a calendar to keep track of your periods. Then you will know when to expect the next one.

Although the time of the first menstruation may be as early as age 9 or 10, it may not be until as late as age 17 or 18. After that, you will usually menstruate every four weeks until you are 45–50, unless you are pregnant. When a baby is growing in the uterus, the extra blood and the soft new lining are needed for the baby.

What should I do when I start to menstruate?

You will need something to catch the blood, something soft and absorbent. You can wear a **menstrual pad**, which is placed between the legs inside the panties. Just peel off the protective paper and press the pad into place. Or you can put a **tampon** inside your vagina. A tampon is a small, tight roll of cotton. Pads should be changed several times a day; tampons should be changed every four to six hours and probably should not be used at night. Toxic shock syndrome, a rare but serious illness, can be caused by not changing tampons often enough.

Both tampons and menstrual pads come in different sizes. The smallest size is usually most comfortable for young girls. Packages of 10 or more are sold in most stores. Instructions come in every package. Ladies' restrooms often have coin-operated machines that sell one tampon or one pad at a time.

What if I start to menstruate at school?

Most schools keep a supply of sanitary napkins on hand. The school nurse, the school secretary, or a woman teacher all are likely either to have some or to know where they are.

But my teacher is a man! What will I tell him?

Tell him the truth. It's a normal happening, and he knows all about it. If you just can't do that, ask if you can see a woman teacher about a personal problem. He'll understand.

Will anyone be able to tell that I am menstruating?

How could they tell? Of course, it's important to bathe or shower every day. You will soon learn how often you need to change your sanitary napkin or tampon. Wrap used napkins in toilet paper and put them in a waste can, never in a toilet.

When you menstruate, do whatever you usually do. Take gym class, wash your hair, swim (wear a tampon). Some girls have mild pains below their waist or feel a little tired and crabby during the first day or two. These girls might choose to cut down on very active sports, but they will probably find that some exercise makes them feel better.

You can look forward to the day when you begin to menstruate. It's a sign that you are on your way to becoming a woman. Of course, you still have a lot further to go. Your body may be getting ready for motherhood, but your mind and spirit still have a great deal of growing to do. Even more important than the physical changes on the steps toward womanhood are the matters of growing in responsibility, integrity, maturity in decision making, and wisdom as God's Spirit guides you. Talk with your parents about each of these key steps. With God's blessing, you will continue to grow in faith as His own dear child.

How Boys Change

Boys usually have their time of fast growth a couple years later than girls do. A boy may grow very fast for a year or two, then continue to grow more slowly until he is 20 or so.

When a boy begins to grow taller and heavier, other changes take place in his body. Hair grows around his penis and under his arms. His testicles get bigger because they are beginning to make sperm cells.

Most adolescent boys are more comfortable if they wear an **athletic supporter** when they participate in active sports. The athletic supporter (or **jockstrap**) is a kind of underpants. It's elastic. It holds the testicles and penis close to the body, where these sensitive organs are less likely to be hurt.

As time goes on, the boy will notice hair beginning to grow above his upper lip. His voice gradually becomes deeper. His penis becomes bigger, his shoulders broader, and his muscles more powerful. More hair appears on his chin; soon he will be ready to shave for the first time.

An adolescent boy will have **erections** more often than he did when he was little. His penis becomes erect—that is, instead of being limp and soft, it becomes hard and stands out from his body.

Often there is no reason for the erection. It just happens. In a few minutes, the penis goes back to its usual size. As the boy grows older, he will have more control over his penis.

When a boy is somewhere between ages 12 and 15, he is old enough to have **ejaculations**—semen shooting out from his penis. Often this happens when he is asleep. Sometimes it's called a **wet dream** because the boy may have a strange and exciting dream about a girl at the same time. This is a perfectly normal part of growing up. Adolescence is indeed a time of many changes.

> Every good and perfect gift is from above, coming down from the Father of the heavenly lights, who does not change like shifting shadows. (James 1:17)

Dear Lord, some people hate changes, and some people want to change everything. I think a little bit of both might be the best way to go.

Some things don't need to change and maybe should not be changed. Some things change, whether we like it or not. And some things, when changed, are corrected, refreshed, or otherwise made beter. Help me to be wise and understanding about the changes in my life.

Lead me to remember that in all circumstances You are with me and that You never change. As the Bible says, "Jesus Christ is the same yesterday and today and forever" (Hebrews 13:8). Your forgiveness, love, compassion, and blessing are constant.

Some things change too much, and some things don't change enough. But there is one change I can be certain of. Because of Jesus Christ, I know that on His return, "the trumpet will sound, the dead will be raised imperishable, and we will be changed" (1 Corinthians 15:52). I can celebrate now because on that day I will have a perfect body—not too small, not too big, not too weak—I will be made perfect as You always intended me to be! Thank You for the perfect life I will have in heaven eternally through Jesus!

6
Am I Normal?

Nearly everyone asks this question while they are growing up. Eleven-year-old Beth feels like a freak because she is taller than her 12-year-old brother, Steve. He doesn't like it either. Beth feels like a giant because she is taller than any of her friends. She doesn't like being the only girl in her class who wears a bra.

Both Beth and Steve should try hard to be patient. In a few years, Beth might be no taller than she is now, and Steve might be tall enough to be a basketball star. They are both normal and have been all along.

Different Rates of Growth

Beth and Steve might feel better if they knew that everyone's growth is controlled by a tiny organ called the **pituitary gland**. The pituitary gland is something like an automatic timer. It sends chemicals called **hormones** into the body. One hormone controls the way bones grow. Another controls changes in a person's sexual organs.

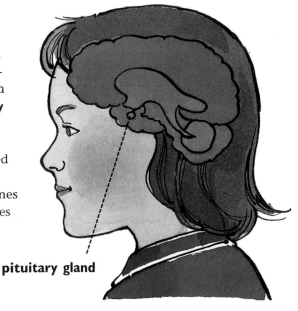

pituitary gland

Each person's growth timer is set a little differently. You might begin the changes of adolescence anytime from 9 until 14. In fact, there are some cases of people who begin even earlier or even later. The average girl will do her growing about two years before the average boy. There is so much variety among normal children, though, that a boy might enter adolescence before his twin sister.

Most people would rather do this extra growing at exactly the same time as their friends. Both early growers and late growers sometimes feel out of the ordinary during the time they are different from their friends. If this happens to you, try to be content with your own rate of growth. It is right for you.

Temporary Problems

Chances are you look very different now than you did a year or two ago. It might be a little hard for you to get used to being so much taller and heavier than you were. Since hands and feet grow first, young people often feel awkward and out of proportion. Muscles don't usually develop as fast as bones do, so they end up trying to make an adult-size body work with child-size muscles. Hard though it is, the best thing you can do is laugh at these problems as you notice them in your body, remembering that they don't last long.

Many girls and boys worry about the weight they gain at this age. Others have the opposite problem. They get tall so fast they don't grow sideways at all! Both the chubby look and the skinny look will go away in time if they exercise and eat the right foods.

Different Shapes and Sizes

Adolescent girls often worry about the size and shape of their breasts. Boys often worry about the size and shape of their testicles and penis. "Am I normal?" they wonder.

Normal people come in many different shapes and sizes. Even in the same person, one breast (or one testicle) may be bigger than the other.

Think how uninteresting life would be if everyone looked exactly alike! Instead, God has made each one of us special in some way. Each of us has something we don't like about ourselves. But we also are blessed with unique abilities and gifts.

You have a choice. You can spend your life unhappy about something you cannot change. Or you can make the most of the good gifts God has given you. Why not appreciate God's blessings that make you who you are?

> Do you not know that your body is a temple of the Holy Spirit within you, whom you have from God? You are not your own, for you were bought with a price. So glorify God in your body. (1 Corinthians 6:19–20 ESV)

Jesus, did You ever worry about growing up? I want to be older, to be powerful and adventurous and independent—but I'm afraid. Now that I see my body beginning to change, half of me would like to keep on being a child.

What will my life be like when I grow up? How will I ever make the right choices? What if I make a mistake?

Put Your hand on my shoulder, Jesus, when I feel panicky about the future. Remind me that You were my age once and that You understand how I feel.

Remind me that one part of my future is sure: You will be there. If I make a mistake, You will forgive me and help me learn from it. You have promised to be with the people who love You. Right now, You are closer to me than I can imagine.

With Your help, I can respect and care for the wonderful body You have given me. Help me to rely on Your power as I think and speak and grow and love. Remind me of Your promise, "I, the LORD, your God, hold your right hand; it is I who say to you, 'Fear not, I am the one who helps you'" (Isaiah 41:13 ESV).

7

Feeling Good about Your Sexuality

Yesterday at a friend's house I saw a TV show I had never seen before. It was sort of funny, but I feel dirty and uneasy now whenever I think about it. I know there were jokes and pictures that were wrong and not God pleasing.

Jesus chose you to be His. What choices will you make as His child? You can choose between feeling good or bad about your body. You can choose TV shows, movies, books, Web sites, and magazines that give you good feelings about yourself and other people—or you can fill your mind and heart with garbage. When you watch or buy things that are sinful, you are sharing and supporting that sin.

But everyone will make fun of me if I don't want to watch that show!

Maybe—but maybe not. Chances are that you weren't the only one who felt uncomfortable. Think about the friends you were with. Which one (or ones) probably felt as you did? What else could you suggest doing instead of watching that improper TV show?

Sometimes it may happen that you are the only one who is mature enough to understand that the group has made a bad choice. Then real courage is needed. "Be watchful, stand firm in the faith . . . be strong. Let all that you do be done in love" (1 Corinthians 16:13–14 ESV). Remember that there are other kids out there who feel just as you do. Your leadership may help your current friends to change. If not, maybe you need to find some new friends.

I don't think I can handle any more teasing than I already get. I'm fat, ugly, and sexually more developed than anyone else in my class. Help!

The kids who tease you probably do not feel good about themselves either. Insecure and immature people often try to make themselves feel better by putting down someone else. Ignoring them is probably the best way to get them to stop teasing you.

Many attractive, successful adults have felt just as "ugly" as you do. Growing up can be very painful at times. If you take care of your body and have a smile that shows a sincere interest in other people, you will become more attractive to others.

What if someone makes you do something bad? My friend Betsy knows she shouldn't let other people touch her private sexual areas—but her teenage cousin has been making her do things she knows are wrong. I said, "Tell your mother," but Betsy says her mom never believes her about anything. How can I help Betsy?

You already have helped Betsy by being her friend. Make sure that she knows that you still like her. Listen sympathetically to what she tells you, but don't embarrass her by asking for details. Promise her that you won't pass her secret on to the other kids. And tell her to say NO to her cousin.

Try to get Betsy to tell an adult she can trust. This adult will talk with Betsy's parents for her. You can help Betsy figure out what to say when she goes for help. You could offer to go with her to see the school nurse or a special teacher.

But what if she has promised not to tell?

It's okay to tell bad secrets, even if you have promised not to. Betsy needs help—and so does her cousin. Explain to Betsy that if someone touches her in a way that doesn't feel right, telling someone she trusts is the best choice for everybody. Such behavior is inappropriate, and the person must be made to stop.

Sometimes it's hard to know whom to trust. Some girls at school were talking about the gym teacher. They said he touched them in a bad way. Should I believe them?

Kids don't usually make up a story like that, but once in a while someone spreads a lie just for excitement or revenge. Of course that's a cruel thing to do. Don't pass the rumor on—but do tell your parents right away.

If you have reasons for doubting whether the story is true, tell your parents why you think it might be false.

My parents sometimes warn me about mixed-up people who are dangerous because they like to hurt kids. I feel really scared sometimes.

It's normal to feel scared sometimes. The thing to remember is that there are lots more good people than bad people. Still, it's smart to plan what you would do to get out of danger. Talk to your parents about how to stay safe around strangers and how to deal with family members or acquaintances who act improperly.

Remember, too, that God will always be there for you in any kind of trouble. He will help you be braver and wiser than you ever thought you could be.

My parents also warn me about smoking, alcohol, and drugs. But my friend says, "It's my body! It's nobody else's business what I put in it."

If you are a Christian, God's Spirit lives in your body. You are a valuable member of God's family. Of course it matters what you put into your body! Remember, "You are not your own, for you were bought with a price. So glorify God in your body" (1 Corinthians 6:19–20 ESV).

Excessive use of alcohol and drug abuse do permanent damage to brain cells. They interfere with a person's thinking and cause him or her to do really stupid things.

Smoking can lead to serious problems such as lung cancer and heart disease. It also makes a person less attractive. Have you ever smelled a smoker's breath? It's awful.

Other people are affected by the choices you make about your body. Mothers who smoke, drink alcohol, or do drugs are much more likely than those who don't to bear children who have serious physical and mental problems. Likewise, children who grow up in homes where adults smoke suffer the physical effects of secondhand smoke. Cigarette smoke, before or after birth, causes tiny infants to gasp for air. It can cause ear infections and lung or breathing problems in older children who are near the smoker. Those who abuse alcohol and drugs often cause accidents that harm others. As a preoccupation with alcohol and drugs takes control of them, they waste their lives, are unproductive, and destroy their relationships. Support of an illegal drug culture leads to many other terrible crimes.

As the Holy Spirit works through God's Word, He gives us the power to honor God in the choices we make about what we put into our bodies and how we care for them. He helps us to live our life for Jesus—the one who lived, died, and now lives again for us!

> We are the temple of the living God. As God has said: "I will live with them and walk among them, and I will be their God, and they will be My people." (2 Corinthians 6:16)

Dear Lord, why is it that some people think that anything about sex is dirty? After all, sex is something You created as a blessing. I guess sin and sinful people can dirty and destroy any of Your blessings to us.

Contrary to what people in the world may tell us to do, nowhere in the Bible do You tell me to go ahead and do whatever I want as long as it's fun and feels good; nowhere do You tell me to follow what my friends or everybody else is doing, even when I know it is wrong; and nowhere do You tell me to use or abuse people by laughing at them or mocking them.

Lead me to honor my body, to respect others, and in all things to give glory to You, dear God. Make me strong to remember the words You say in the Bible, such as "Honor one another above yourselves" (Romans 12:10), "Encourage one another and build each other up" (1 Thessalonians 5:11), and "Show proper respect to everyone" (1 Peter 2:17).

When I am tempted to act in ways that do not please You—in the way I dress, the words I say, the Web sites I search, the movies I watch, or the books I read—help me fight temptation and focus on whatever You would have me do.

You even tell me what those "whatevers" are: "whatever is true, whatever is noble, whatever is right, whatever is pure, whatever is lovely, whatever is admirable—if anything is excellent or praiseworthy—think about such things" (Philippians 4:8).

8

It's Great to Be Alive!

When God finished making the world, He looked at it and saw that it was good. He had made many, many different kinds of plants and animals. Each one was valuable in its own way.

God made each living thing able to bring new life into the world. Each is able to **reproduce** itself—to make more of its own kind.

Some flowers, for instance, reproduce when bees bring pollen (a yellow powder) from one flower to another. The pollen is like sperm cells. Seeds are formed when pollen joins the egg cells in the center of a flower.

A female fish lays many eggs in the water. The male fish swims over them and sprinkles them with sperm cells. New life begins wherever an egg and a sperm join.

Other animals reproduce very much as humans do. For instance, male dogs, elephants, and mice all have penises, which they use to place sperm inside the females.

But animals cannot love their mates in the way that humans do. They cannot have the same respect and care for each other. They can never have the joy humans find in a loving and caring marriage.

Animals often take very good care of their babies—for a while. Mother elephants take care of their babies for four years—much longer than most other animal mothers. But human babies need much more care, love, and teaching than any animal. They need parents who are able to make wise decisions, parents who can give them a good home for many years, parents who help them grow in the love and nurture of God's grace. (Read Deuteronomy 11:18–19.)

It takes a long time to grow up enough to be a good parent. Even for an adult, it's not an easy job. All parents make mistakes—sometimes serious ones.

It's a good thing that God has special love for the people He made. What would we do if Jesus had not lived and died for us? Christian parents and children know that God forgives their mistakes for Jesus' sake. They know that God can and will help when trouble comes.

If you have children of your own someday, you will find great joy in loving and caring for them. You will have used God's good gift of sex to bring very special people into the world. By your love and care, you can show your children a little of what God's love is like.

God's love can make sex a wonderful part of your love for another person. Guided by Him, you can choose a husband who will share your life. The love you have for each other will be extra-special if God lives in both of you.

That time seems a long way in the future, doesn't it? The growing years ahead of you are also God's gift—your time to get ready for adult life. You will learn to make good decisions, remembering that you are God's child. You can stay close to Jesus by reading and hearing about Him—and talking to Him in prayer. That way you can grow in faith and in your faith life every day. You can discover good ways to use all the wonderful gifts He has given you.

Following God's will always, you'll be able to say, "It's good to be alive!"

Consider yourselves . . . alive to God in Christ Jesus. (Romans 6:11 ESV)

Lord, as I grow and change, I know there are a lot of "don'ts" to consider and rules to obey. Help me to see these not so much as limitations but as guidelines for living as Your redeemed and sanctified child. You know what is best for me, and You want what is best for me. You gave me Your very best in Your Son, Jesus!

I need Your forgiveness when I am weak and Your enabling power to make me strong. Lead me to live as Your child. Keep before me the Good News that because Jesus died on the cross and "was raised from the dead through the glory of the Father, we too may live a new life" (Romans 6:4). I know this new life in Christ is not the easy way, but I also know You will enable me to live through the power of the Holy Spirit.

When I'm unsure what this new life looks like or what I should do, point me to Your Word, which tells me that it is a life growing fruitfully in "love, joy, peace, patience, kindness, goodness, faithfulness, gentleness and self-control" (Galatians 5:22–23).

Some Words Used in This Book

adolescence (a-doh-LES-sense) The years when a person changes from a child to an adult.

anus (AY-nes) The opening where bowel movements leave the body.

athletic supporter (ath-LEH-tik suh-PORT-er) Elastic underwear for boys that holds the penis and testicles close to the body. (See **jockstrap**.)

characteristics (kar-ik-tuh-RISS-tiks) The traits or qualities that make a person or thing special. A good singing voice, long legs, and brown eyes are characteristics a person might have.

circumcision (sur-kum-SIZH-un) A minor operation in which the loose skin, or foreskin, is removed from the end of the penis.

ejaculation (ee-jack-yoo-LAY-shun) A discharge (coming out) of semen from the penis.

erection (ee-RECK-shun) A time when the penis is stiff and stands out from the body.

fallopian tube (fal-LOW-pee-an tube) The tube inside a woman's body that provides a passage for the egg cell from the ovary to the uterus.

fraternal twins (fruh-TUR-n'l twins) Twins who grew from two different egg cells that were joined by two different sperm cells.

gene (JEEN) A tiny part of a sperm cell or egg cell that carries characteristics from the father or the mother.

hormones (HOR-mones) Chemicals that control growth or other changes in the body.

identical twins (eye-DEN-ti-k'l twins) Twins who grew from one egg cell that divided in two after it was joined by one sperm cell.

incubator (IN-kyoo-bay-ter) A glassed-in bed, specially equipped for babies who were born too soon and need extra care.

intercourse (IN-ter-kors) The act in which sperm cells leave a man's body and enter a woman's body.

jockstrap (JOCK-strap) An athletic supporter; elastic underwear that holds the penis and testicles close to the body.

menstrual pad (men-stroo-al pad) A soft pad used to catch the unneeded blood, etc., that flows from a woman's uterus during menstruation.

menstruation (men-stroo-AY-shun) The monthly flow through the vagina of unneeded blood and tissue from the uterus.

organ (OR-gun) A part of the body that has a particular job to do.

ovary (OH-vuh-ree) The female organ in which egg cells develop and grow.

penis (PEE-niss) The male organ through which both urine and semen leave the body.

period (PEER-ee-ud) The regular monthly time during which a woman menstruates, usually three to seven days.

pituitary gland (pih-TYOO-ih-ter-ee gland) The tiny group of cells that makes hormones controlling body growth and the work of many organs in the body.

placenta (pluh-SEN-tuh) A special organ that develops on the wall of the uterus during pregnancy. The placenta helps food and oxygen move from the mother's bloodstream to the baby's bloodstream and carries wastes from the baby to the mother.

pregnant (PREG-n'nt) Carrying a growing baby in the uterus.

premature (pree-muh-TYOOR) Born too early, before the usual nine months of growing in the uterus has passed.

reproduce (ree-proh-DOOS) To make more of the same kind.

reproductive organs (ree-proh-DUK-tiv OR-guns) The parts of the body used to create babies. In a boy, these include testicles, scrotum, and penis. In a girl, these include ovaries, fallopian tubes, uterus, vagina, and vulva.

scrotum (SKROH-t'm) The bag of skin in which the testicles hang between the legs of a male.

semen (SEE-m'n) A milky liquid that has sperm cells in it.

sex (SEKS) Male or female. Word used to identify the reproductive act.

sexual organs (SEKS-shoo-ul organs) The body organs needed for reproduction, the creation of new life.

tampon (TAM-pahn) An absorbent plug placed in the vagina to catch unneeded blood, etc., that flows from a woman's uterus during menstruation.

testicle (TESS-ti-k'l) The male organ in which sperm cells grow.

uterus (YOO-ter-us) The female organ inside which a baby grows.

vagina (vuh-JY-nuh) A tunnel leading from the uterus to the outside of the body.

vulva (VUL-vuh) The folds of skin and flesh that protect the opening to the vagina.

wet dream A dream during which semen comes out of the penis.

womb (WOOM) Uterus, the female organ inside which a baby grows.